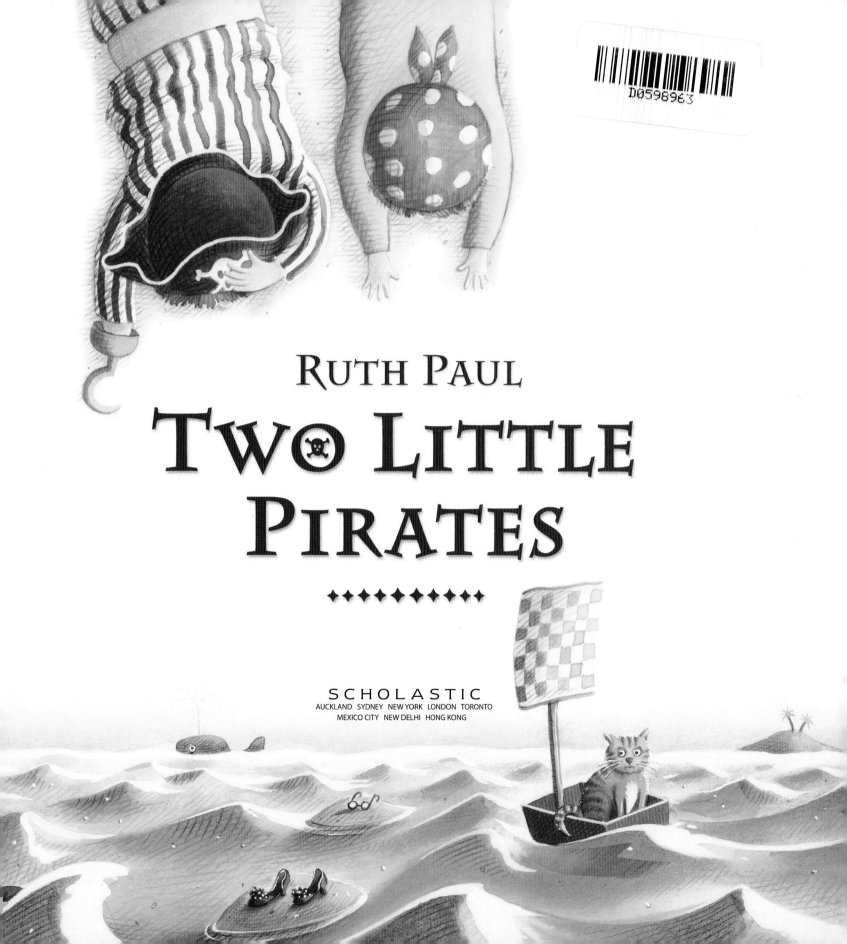

# Ruth Paul
# Two Little Pirates

SCHOLASTIC
AUCKLAND SYDNEY NEW YORK LONDON TORONTO
MEXICO CITY NEW DELHI HONG KONG

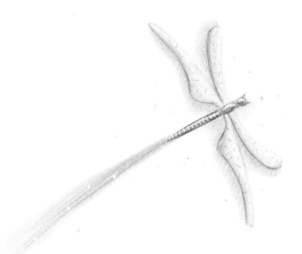

The dawn slips in on a dragonfly's wing,
in through a porthole to wake up the King,
and in through the misty remains of the night,
come two little pirates preparing to fight.

They circle the ship, they swing up their ropes,
they scramble aboard with a swag full of hopes.

With gaps in their teeth and sticky-out hair,
they leap from the rigging and sail through the air.

They jump, they spin, they roar and they whack.
They holler and hoot as they launch their attack.

They capture the slumbering Queen by surprise,
foolishly blind to the glint in her eyes.
They tease and torment her and, under the sheet,
they wickedly, horridly, tickle her feet.

The King is alerted by all the kerfuffle.
He leaps to his feet to join in the scuffle.
He fights with a fury, ferocious and rotten,
but trips on a pirate and lands on his bottom.

They punch, they jump, they wriggle and kick.
They're awfully rough and amazingly quick.

"Avast!" the King roars. "Ahoy and ahoo!
I'll have you made into pirate-boy stew!"

"Alas!" squeals the Queen "I wouldn't eat that.
They've too many bones and not enough fat!"

The pirates laugh at their doolally rants,
but the King catches one by the seat of his pants!
On the toe of the other the Queen takes a grip,
and they dangle them both from the side of the ship.

They squeal, they squirm, they bellow and bark …
they don't seem to like being fed to a shark.

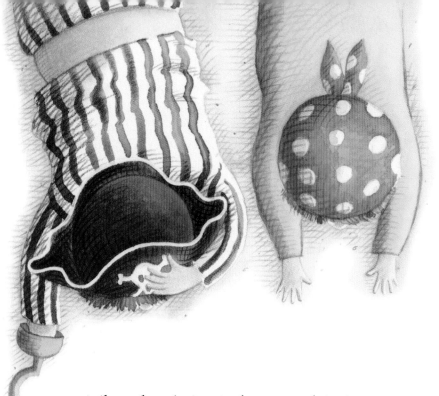

The shark isn't happy, his jaws snap shut,
pirates that loud are a pain in the gut.

"A-haaaaarrrgh!" they roar.

"Afoul!" cries the King.
"A fate worse than bait?
I've got just the thing."

"You'll work for your living! You'll scrub all the decks,
you'll shine all the brass, you'll massage our necks."

"Agreed!" says the Queen. "You'll wash all the sails,
and when you've done that, you can polish my nails."

They moan, they dawdle, they squabble and scowl.
Tidying up is a punishment foul.

When all is in order, shipshape and spruce,
two little pirates agree to a truce.

They'll use good manners, they won't stomp their feet …
in exchange for a cuddle and something to eat.

Shipmates together, they stand down from duty.
Two little pirates are counting their booty.

Brave buccaneers for a few moments more,
the tide pulls them in to the bright morning shore.

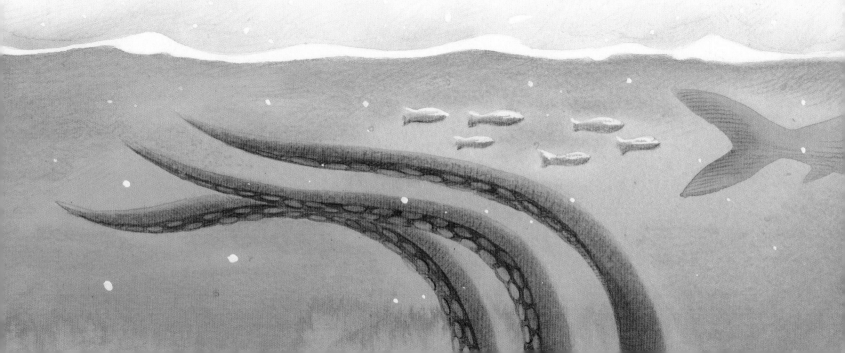

They yawn, they stretch, they snuggle and squeeze,
as day breaks over the wide open seas.

FOR MY OWN TWO LITTLE PIRATES,
IN MEMORY OF THE LOST SLEEP-IN.

First published in 2010 by Scholastic New Zealand Limited
Private Bag 94407, Botany, Manukau 2163, New Zealand

Scholastic Australia Pty Limited, PO Box 579, Gosford, NSW 2250, Australia

Scholastic Canada Ltd, 175 Hillmount Road, Markham, Ontario L6C 1Z7, Canada

Text and illustrations © Ruth Paul 2010

ISBN 978-1-86943-935-4

National Library of New Zealand Cataloguing-in-Publication Data

---

Paul, Ruth.
Two little pirates / Ruth Paul.
ISBN 978-1-86943-935-4
[1. Pirates—Fiction. 2. Play—Fiction. 3. Stories in rhyme.] I. Title.
NZ823.3—dc 22

---

12 11 10 9 8 7 6 5 4 3 2 1                    0 1 2 3 4 5 6 7/1

Illustrations created in watercolour and colour pencil.

Publishing team: Diana Murray, Penny Scown and Annette Bisman
Design: Vida Kelly
Typeset in Old Claude